A

for a Boy

INTRO TO PHASE 5

/oy/

Level 4+
Blue+

BookLife Readers

Helpful Hints for Reading at Home

The graphemes (written letters) and phonemes (units of sound) used throughout this series are aligned with Letters and Sounds. This offers a consistent approach to learning whether reading at home or in the classroom.

THIS BLUE+ BOOK BAND SERVES AS AN INTRODUCTION TO PHASE 5. EACH BOOK IN THIS BAND USES ALL PHONEMES LEARNED UP TO PHASE 4, WHILE INTRODUCING ONE PHASE 5 PHONEME. HERE IS A LIST OF PHONEMES FOR THIS PHASE, WITH THE NEW PHASE 5 PHONEME. AN EXAMPLE OF THE PRONUNCIATION CAN BE FOUND IN BRACKETS.

Phase 3			
j (jug)	v (van)	w (wet)	x (fox)
y (yellow)	z (zoo)	zz (buzz)	qu (quick)
ch (chip)	sh (shop)	th (thin/then)	ng (ring)
ai (rain)	ee (feet)	igh (night)	oa (boat)
oo (boot/look)	ar (farm)	or (for)	ur (hurt)
ow (cow)	oi (coin)	ear (dear)	air (fair)
ure (sure)	er (corner)		

New Phase 5 Phoneme	oy (boy, toy, joy)

HERE ARE SOME WORDS WHICH YOUR CHILD MAY FIND TRICKY.

Phase 4 Tricky Words			
said	were	have	there
like	little	so	one
do	when	some	out
come	what		

TOP TIPS FOR HELPING YOUR CHILD TO READ:

- Allow children time to break down unfamiliar words into units of sound and then encourage children to string these sounds together to create the word.
- Encourage your child to point out any focus phonics when they are used.
- Read through the book more than once to grow confidence.
- Ask simple questions about the text to assess understanding.
- Encourage children to use illustrations as prompts.

INTRO TO PHASE 5

/oy/

This book introduces the phoneme /oy/ and is a Blue+ Level 4+ book band.

A Toy for a Boy

Written by
Robin Twiddy

Illustrated by
Simona Hodonova

"I need a toy," yells the boy. "Bring me a toy!"

The men of the land all bring him toys.
Little toys and big toys.

This man has got a cap gun. Will the boy enjoy the cap gun?

Bang, bang, then into the bin. The boy did not enjoy the toy.

"Destroy the toy," yells the boy.
"And send the man to the stocks."

The next man steps into the room.
He has a big bag.

"It is a doll," mutters the man.
"I do not need a doll," yells the boy.

"But it is a troll's doll!" booms the man as he tugs the bag down.

The boy tugs at the doll, but it will not shift.

"Destroy the doll!" yells the boy.
"Send this man to the stocks!"

The next man has a thing the boy has not seen.

"This thing will bring you joy," this man tells the boy.

But the toy is not bringing joy to the boy.
It annoys the boy.

"Send this man to the stocks and destroy this toy!" howls the boy.

The next man enters the room. He has blocks in a bag.

The man looks at the boy, the toys, his blocks and the stocks.

"I will get in the stocks," sighs the man.
"Destroy the toy!" yells the boy.

"I bring you the best toy." The next man winks. He brings a toy that looks just like him.

"I do not like this man," yells the boy. "Destroy his toy. Send him to the stocks."

"Next," snaps the boy, but there are not a lot of men left.

"I bring you milk caps," the man tells the boy. He has a stack of card discs.

"They are just card discs," groans the boy. "That is not a toy!"

"Destroy his discs," yells the boy, "and send him to the stocks!"

"Bring in the next toy," orders the boy.
Will the boy enjoy this toy?

"This is the toy that you need," the queen tells her boy.

"My ted! I lost him as a little boy."
The boy hugs the queen tight.

A Toy for a Boy

1) Where are the men sent if the boy does not like their toy?

2) What was the second toy that was shown to the boy?

a) Skipping rope

b) Computer game

c) Doll

3) Why do you think the boy is important?

4) Do you like the boy? Why or why not?

5) Can you think of a better toy that you would bring to the boy? Why?

King's Lynn, Norfolk PE30 4LS

ISBN 978-1-80155-056-7

A catalogue record for this book is available from the British Library.

A Toy for a Boy
Written by Robin Twiddy
Illustrated by Simona Hodonova

An Introduction to BookLife Readers...

Our Readers have been specifically created in line with the London Institute of Education's approach to book banding and are phonetically decodable and ordered to support each phase of the Letters and Sounds document.

Each book has been created to provide the best possible reading and learning experience. Our aim is to share our love of books with children, providing both emerging readers and prolific page-turners with beautiful books that are guaranteed to provoke interest and learning, regardless of ability.

BOOK BAND GRADED using the Institute of Education's approach to levelling.

PHONETICALLY DECODABLE supporting each phase of Letters and Sounds.

EXERCISES AND QUESTIONS to offer reinforcement and to ascertain comprehension.

BEAUTIFULLY ILLUSTRATED to inspire and provoke engagement, providing a variety of styles for the reader to enjoy whilst reading through the series.

AUTHOR INSIGHT:
ROBIN TWIDDY

Robin Twiddy is one of BookLife Publishing's most creative and prolific editorial talents, who imbues all his copy with a sense of adventure and energy. Robin's Cambridge-based first class honours degree in psychosocial studies offers a unique viewpoint on factual information and allows him to relay information in a manner that readers of any age are guaranteed to retain. He also holds a certificate in Teaching in the Lifelong Sector, and a postgraduate certificate in Consumer Psychology.

A father of two, Robin has written over 70 titles for BookLife and specialises in conceptual, role-playing narratives which promote interaction with the reader and inspire even the most reluctant of readers to fully engage with his books.

INTRO TO PHASE 5

/oy/

This book introduces the phoneme /oy/ and is a Blue+ Level 4+ book band.